CLOTHING, COSTUMES, and UNIFORMS

Throughout

AMERICAN HISTORY™

What People Wore
in
Colonial America

∞ Allison Stark Draper ∞

The Rosen Publishing Group's

PowerKids Press™

New York

For my mother

Published in 2001 by The Rosen Publishing Group, Inc.
29 East 21st Street, New York, NY 10010

First Edition

Book Design: Emily Muschinske

Photo Credits: title page, p. 7, 10 © Bettmann/CORBIS; pp. 5, 7, 16, 17, 22 courtesy of *Historic Dress in America* by Elizabeth McClellan/illustrations © Sophie B. Steel; pp. 5, 9, 11, 13 (painting by Paul Elie Ranson), 19 (painting by Junius Brutus Stearns) © SuperStock; p. 13 (photo) © Catherine Karnow/CORBIS; p. 15, 22 © Archive Photos; p. 15 (reenactment photos) © Jeffrey Foxx; p. 21 © North Wind Picture Archives; p. 22 (pudding cap) © www.history.org

Manufactured in the United States of America

Contents

Coming to America

Starting in the 1600s, many people left England to settle **colonies** in America. Some left so they could **worship** God the way they chose. Others left to make money. At this time, rich people in England wore the same style of clothes as the king and queen. Their clothes were made out of costly fabrics, like silk and lace. They wore gold buttons and wide, stiff collars called ruffs. When people began making money in America, they dressed like wealthy people in England.

The **Puritans** were a religious group in England that came to America. Puritans thought religious people should dress in plain clothing without lace or other fancy trim. The Puritan way of dressing was popular for almost 100 years.

The Puritans' clothes did not have the bright ribbons or lace trim of the rich farmers' clothes. Colonial men wore leather shoes with brass, steel, or silver buckles. They wore wheels called spurs on their heels to guide their horses along when riding.

Puritan Fashions

Puritan men and women wore black hats with wide brims and high **crowns**. These hats were called sugarloaf hats. Puritan men wore their hair short. They wore dark, plain coats and wool stockings. Puritan women wore dark gowns with stiff underskirts. Puritans in the Massachusetts Bay Colony passed laws about clothes. They did not allow people to wear new clothes from Europe. People could not wear silver or gold jewelry. They could not wear short sleeves. As Massachusetts got bigger, some of these laws became less firm. Massachusetts still had more laws than other colonies, though. People rarely wore the wigs, makeup, and wooden false teeth that were popular elsewhere.

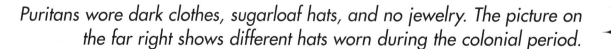

Puritans wore dark clothes, sugarloaf hats, and no jewelry. The picture on the far right shows different hats worn during the colonial period.

The Quaker Way of Dressing

Some colonists settled in an area called the Delaware Bay. These people were known as **Quakers**. The Quakers thought that fancy clothes would make people forget about religion and the work they had to do. Quaker men wore heavy **breeches** and plain coats. They kept their hair short and did not wear the powdered wigs that were in style at the time. They wore plain, round hats. Women wore slim, simple dresses. Over the dresses, they wore white or colored aprons. Quaker women wore hoods or sugarloaf hats. Women were not supposed to wear gold or fancy jewelry. They did not have lace or other decoration on their clothing.

Quaker women wore dresses without lace or other fancy trim on them.

Virginia Farmers and Country People

There were many rich farmers in the colony of Virginia. Rich Virginians wore suits and dresses made of fancy cloth, like silk or linen. They wore silk stockings and pearl necklaces. Wealthy Virginians wore wide cuffs on their clothes. They wore feathers in their hats. Both men and women wore high heels on their shoes.

This picture shows rich men and women from Virginia. They dressed in fine fabrics that showed off their wealth.

Workers and country people dressed much more plainly. Women wore straight skirts that came down to their ankles. They wore **bodices** that laced up in the back. Women protected their clothes by covering them with aprons. Working men wore breeches. They wore leather vests or aprons over their shirts. This helped protect them as they did their work.

The children in these photos are wearing the plain dress of colonial country people. The girls wore aprons to protect their dresses.

Homemade Clothes

In colonial America, only rich people wore clothes made from European **patterns**. Most Americans made their own clothes. They raised sheep and **sheared** them for wool. They spun the wool into yarn. People knitted the yarn into stockings and caps. The yarn was also woven into cloth on machines called **looms**. The cloth was then sewn into clothes. Colonial Americans used thread made from a plant called flax.

The Puritans and Quakers did not believe in wearing bright colors. Many Americans liked to wear bright colors, though. They gathered plants to make colorful dyes. They used goldenrod and birchbark to make yellow dye. Pokeberry made red dye and indigo made blue dye. People boiled the plants in big pots. Then they stirred in the clothes to color them.

Plants, such as goldenrod, were used to make dyes for clothes. This woman is spinning wool into yarn.

Gowns and Corsets

In the early 1600s, women wore narrow gowns. They wore wide collars that covered their shoulders. Starting in the late 1600s, women slit their overskirts in front and drew them back like curtains. They did this to show off their **petticoats**. Then they pulled the two sides back farther to make a **bustle**. As time went on, skirts got wider and wider. The skirts were sewn over panniers. Panniers were hoops that supported a skirt on either side of a woman's body. The **corsets** women wore got tighter and tighter. They made women's waists look very small. From the waist up, women's clothes were more practical. For example, for activities like riding or walking they wore comfortable coats that were like men's coats.

These three pictures show a woman pulling back her skirt to form a bustle. ➔✣

Women wore tight corsets to make their waists look as small as possible. Sometimes the corsets were so tight that they made women feel faint.

Jackets and Wigs

Starting in the 1600s, men began to wear suits. They wore long jackets. The jackets had wide cuffs and **pleats** in the back. Men wore the jackets unbuttoned over long, buttoned vests. They wore loose, comfortable breeches. They wore scarves around their necks. As time went on, vests and jackets got shorter. Breeches got tighter and fancier. By 1710, rich men were also wearing high wigs. The wigs were powdered white. It was uncomfortable to wear a tall hat over these wigs. For this reason, hats got shorter. These shorter hats had broad rims. The rims were also curved.

Many colonial men wore high, powdered wigs. They wore short hats over the wigs so they would be comfortable.

16

The wealthy man on the right has on a long jacket, a vest, and a high, powdered wig. The woman is wearing a silk dress and petticoats. She has on panniers to make her dress look wide.

Red and Blue Uniforms

The English controlled the army in colonial America. The American and English soldiers who fought in the army fought for the English king. The English soldiers wore red uniforms. The American soldiers in the king's army wore uniforms that stood for their colonies. Each colony had its own uniform.

In 1754, George Washington fought for the English in a war against the French. Washington would later lead the colonies as they fought for freedom from English rule. During the war against the French, Washington led soldiers in Virginia. The soldiers wore blue uniforms. The red and blue uniforms were easily spotted by the Native Americans who were fighting alongside the French. The Native Americans wore deerskin, which made them hard for the colonists to see.

George Washington, shown on horseback, is wearing the blue uniform of Virginia. English soldiers wore red uniforms.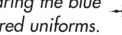

The Abenaki

One Native American tribe that lived in northern New England was the Abenaki. The Abenaki wore clothes made of deerskin or moose hide. They decorated their clothes with porcupine **quills** and moose hair. Men wore breechcloths and leather belts. When it was cold, they wore leggings. Women wore knee-length skirts and leggings. Both men and women wore fur robes. When the English came to America, the Abenaki started to use the woolen cloth that the English gave them. They began to use glass beads to decorate their deerskin. The Abenaki changed the way the English dressed, too. The English started to wear fur capes and fur blankets in the winter. They also started to wear more **buckskin**.

Tribes such as the Abenaki wore breechcloths, leggings, and leather belts.

Little Grown-Ups

   In colonial times, both boys and girls wore dresses until they were five or six. These dresses had bodices like the ones on women's dresses. Toddlers wore padded caps called pudding caps that protected their heads if they fell. Pudding caps were made out of velvet, horsehair stuffing, and leather. As children got older, they dressed like their parents. Girls wore corsets and petticoats under their dresses. Little boys wore breeches like their fathers. This was seen as a boy's first step toward manhood.

pudding cap

Once a girl reached the age of five or six, she began dressing like an adult. She wore dresses with tight bodices, corsets, and petticoats.

Glossary

bodices (BOD-is-ez) The upper parts of women's dresses.

breeches (BREE-chez) Short pants that cover the hips and thighs.

buckskin (BUK-skin) A strong, soft leather made from the skins of deer.

bustle (BUH-sul) A pillow of fabric on the back of a woman's dress, just below the waist.

colonies (KAH-luh-neez) Areas in a new country where a large group of people live that are still ruled by the leaders and laws of their old country.

corsets (KOR-sets) Stiff pieces of women's underwear that tied tightly around the ribs, waist, and hips.

crowns (KROWNZ) The parts of hats that cover the top of the head.

looms (LOOMZ) Devices for weaving yarn into cloth.

patterns (PA-terns) Exact plans for making clothes.

petticoats (PEH-tee-kohts) Fluffy underskirts.

pleats (PLEETZ) Folds in a piece of cloth made by doubling the cloth over on itself.

Puritans (PYUR-it-ens) People in the 1500s and 1600s who belonged to the Protestant religion.

Quakers (KWAY-kurz) People who belong to a religion that believes in equality for all people, strong families and communities, and peace.

quills (KWILZ) The hollow, sharp spines from a porcupine.

sheared (SHEERD) When the wool has been cut from a sheep.

worship (WUR-ship) To pay great honor and respect to someone or something.

23

Index

Web Sites

To find out more about what people wore in colonial America check out this Web site:
http://www.history.org/life/clothing/home.html